S0-ADJ-176

ALSO BY LANGSTON HUGHES

———

POETRY
The Weary Blues
Fields of Wonder
Shakespeare in Harlem
One Way Ticket
Selected Poems (1959)

A NOVEL
Not Without Laughter

SHORT STORIES
The Ways of White Folks

AN AUTOBIOGRAPHY
The Big Sea

———

These are Borzoi Books, published by
ALFRED A. KNOPF

THE DREAM KEEPER

And Other Poems

Here is a selection of sixty poems by the famous Negro poet Langston Hughes. The book is divided into five sections arranged according to mood, including short lyrics of great beauty, stanzas in serious vein, rollicking songs, and some very fine Negro blues.

Helen Sewell's black-and-white designs carry out the Negro note with depth and understanding.

THE DREAM KEEPER

AND OTHER POEMS

LANGSTON HUGHES

Illustrations by Helen Sewell

NEW YORK: ALFRED A. KNOPF

DISCARD

50881

THIS IS A BORZOI BOOK PUBLISHED BY ALFRED A. KNOPF, INC.

Introduction copyright © 1986 by Augusta Baker.
Copyright 1932 by Alfred A. Knopf, Inc.
Copyright renewed 1960 by Langston Hughes.
All rights reserved under International and Pan-American Copyright
Conventions. Published in the United States by Alfred A. Knopf, Inc.,
New York, and simultaneously in Canada by Random House of
Canada Limited, Toronto. Originally published in the
United States by Alfred A. Knopf, Inc., New York,
in 1932. Distributed by Random House, Inc., New York.
Manufactured in the United States of America
6 8 0 9 7

Library of Congress Cataloging-in-Publication Data
Hughes, Langston, 1902–1967. The dream keeper and other poems.
Summary: A collection of fifty-nine poems, selected by the
author for young readers, including lyrical poems,
songs, and blues, many exploring the black experience.
1. Children's poetry, American. [1. Afro-Americans—Poetry.
2. American poetry—Afro-American authors] I. Sewell, Helen,
1896–1957, ill. II. Title. PS3515.U274D7 1986 811'.52 85-19762
ISBN 0-394-91096-6 (lib. bdg.)

TO MY BROTHER

The author wishes to thank the editors of the various magazines, including *The New Republic, Survey Graphic, Vanity Fair, The Crisis, Opportunity*, and *The World Tomorrow* for their permission in reprinting certain of these poems.

CONTENTS

DRESSED UP

FEET O' JESUS

WALKERS WITH THE DAWN

Introduction

My late husband was an instructor at Lincoln University in Pennsylvania in 1927. Langston Hughes, a published poet who had won prizes for his writing, decided to earn a college degree and so he found himself, at age 25, in what must have been a boring English class. The instructor (my husband-to-be) asked to see a book in which Langston was writing. It was his French-English dictionary and on the flyleaf, hastily scrawled, was a beautiful poem:

> Hold fast to dreams
> For if dreams die
> Life is a broken-winged bird
> That cannot fly.

In 1932 *The Dream Keeper* was published, and in it was "my poem" which now had a title—"Dreams." Hughes had selected his poems for young people and he had written them out of his own blackness. Hughes had great pride in his race, and he often said that he wished to give black boys and girls the same pride which he had.

As a children's librarian in the late 1930s, assigned to the 135th Street Branch of the New York Public Library, I had an opportunity to share these poems with the Harlem children as well as with children from other parts of the city. Hughes became a favorite writer with these children, and their favorite poems were "Mother to Son" and "Youth." Today, as I share Hughes's poems, these are still favorites. Hughes was generous with himself, and so he shared his poetry and other writing with groups of young people all over this country and the world. As a writer for adults and children, he left his mark on the literary scene. He died on May 22, 1967. As a friend he will never be replaced.

> I loved my friend.
> He went away from me.
> There's nothing more to say.
> The poem ends,
> Soft as it began—
> I loved my friend.
> —Langston Hughes

AUGUSTA BAKER
Storyteller-in-Residence
University of South Carolina

March, 1986

THE DREAM KEEPER

The Dream Keeper

Bring me all of your dreams,
You dreamers,
Bring me all of your
Heart melodies
That I may wrap them
In a blue cloud-cloth
Away from the too-rough fingers
Of the world.

3

Winter Moon

How thin and sharp is the moon tonight!
How thin and sharp and ghostly white
Is the slim curved crook of the moon tonight!

Fairies

Out of the dust of dreams
Fairies weave their garments.
Out of the purple and rose of old memories
They make rainbow wings.
No wonder we find them such marvellous things!

Autumn Thought

Flowers are happy in summer.
In autumn they die and are blown away.
  Dry and withered,
Their petals dance on the wind
Like little brown butterflies.

Dreams

Hold fast to dreams
For if dreams die
Life is a broken-winged bird
That cannot fly.

Hold fast to dreams
For when dreams go
Life is a barren field
Frozen with snow.

April Rain Song

Let the rain kiss you.
Let the rain beat upon your head with silver liquid drops.
Let the rain sing you a lullaby.

The rain makes still pools on the sidewalk.
The rain makes running pools in the gutter.
The rain plays a little sleep-song on our roof at night—

And I love the rain.

After Many Springs

Now,
In June,
When the night is a vast softness
Filled with blue stars,
And broken shafts of moon-glimmer
Fall upon the earth,
Am I too old to see the fairies dance?
I cannot find them any more.

Winter Sweetness

This little house is sugar.
   Its roof with snow is piled,
And from its tiny window
   Peeps a maple-sugar child.

Quiet Girl

I would liken you
To a night without stars
Were it not for your eyes.
I would liken you
To a sleep without dreams
Were it not for your songs.

Poem

I loved my friend.
He went away from me.
There's nothing more to say.
The poem ends,
Soft as it began—
I loved my friend.

Joy

I went to look for Joy,
Slim, dancing Joy,
Gay, laughing Joy,
Bright-eyed Joy—
And I found her
Driving the butcher's cart
In the arms of the butcher boy!
Such company, such company,
As keeps this young nymph, Joy!

SEA CHARM

Water-Front Streets

The spring is not so beautiful there—
But dream ships sail away
To where the spring is wondrous rare
And life is gay.

The spring is not so beautiful there—
But lads put out to sea
Who carry beauties in their hearts
And dreams, like me.

Long Trip

The sea is a wilderness of waves,
A desert of water.
We dip and dive,
Rise and roll,
Hide and are hidden
On the sea.
  Day, night,
  Night, day,
The sea is a desert of waves,
A wilderness of water.

Sea Calm

How still,
How strangely still
The water is today.
It is not good
For water
To be so still that way.

Sailor

He sat upon the rolling deck
Half a world away from home,
And smoked a Capstan cigarette
And watched the blue waves tipped with foam.

He had a mermaid on his arm,
An anchor on his breast,
And tattooed on his back he had
A blue bird in a nest.

Seascape

Off the coast of Ireland
As our ship passed by
We saw a line of fishing ships
Etched against the sky.

Off the coast of England
As we rode the foam
We saw an Indian merchantman
Coming home.

Mexican Market Woman

This ancient hag
Who sits upon the ground
Selling her scanty wares
Day in, day round,
Has known high wind-swept mountains,
And the sun has made
Her skin so brown.

Beggar Boy

What is there within this beggar lad
That I can neither hear nor feel nor see,
That I can neither know nor understand
And still it calls to me?

Is not he but a shadow in the sun—
A bit of clay, brown, ugly, given life?
And yet he plays upon his flute a wild free tune
As if Fate had not bled him with her knife!

Parisian Beggar Woman

Once you were young.
Now, hunched in the cold,
Nobody cares
That you are old.

Once you were beautiful.
Now, in the street,
No one remembers
Your lips were sweet.

Oh, withered old woman
Of rue Fontaine,
Nobody but death
Will kiss you again.

Irish Wake

In the dark they fell a-crying
For the dead who'd gone away,
And you could hear the drowsy wailing
Of those compelled to stay—
But when the sun rose making
All the dooryard bright and clear
The mourners got up smiling,
Happy they were here.

Death of an Old Seaman

We buried him high on the windy hill,
But his soul went out to sea.
I know, for I heard, when all was still,
His sea-soul say to me:

Put no tombstone at my head,
For here I do not make my bed.
Strew no flowers on my grave,
I've gone back to the wind and wave.
Do not, do not weep for me,
For I am happy with my sea.

Sea Charm

Sea charm
The sea's own children
Do not understand.
They know
But that the sea is strong
Like God's hand.
They know
But that sea wind is sweet
Like God's breath,
And that the sea holds
A wide, deep death.

DRESSED UP

A NOTE ON BLUES

The five poems in this section on pages 36, 37, 40, 44, and 47, are written in the manner of the Negro folk songs known as Blues. The Blues, unlike the Spirituals, have a strict poetic pattern: one long line, repeated, and a third line to rhyme with the first two. Sometimes the second line in repetition is slightly changed and sometimes, but very seldom, it is omitted. Unlike the Spirituals, the Blues are not group songs. When sung under natural circumstances, they are usually sung by one man or one woman alone. Whereas the Spirituals are often songs about escaping from trouble, going to heaven and living happily ever after, the Blues are songs about being in the midst of trouble, friendless, hungry, disappointed in love, right here on earth. The mood of the Blues is almost always despondency, but when they are sung people laugh.

Dressed Up

I had ma clothes cleaned
Just like new.
I put 'em on but
I still feels blue.

I bought a new hat,
Sho is fine,
But I wish I had back that
Old gal o' mine.

I got new shoes—
They don't hurt ma feet,
But I ain't got nobody
For to call me sweet.

Reasons Why

Just because I loves you—
That's de reason why
Ma soul is full of color
Like de wings of a butterfly.

Just because I loves you
That's de reason why
Ma heart's a fluttering aspen leaf
When you pass by.

Negro Dancers

"Me an' ma baby's
Got two mo' ways,
Two mo' ways to do de Charleston!
  Da, da,
   Da, da, da!
Two mo' ways to do de Charleston!"

Soft light on the tables,
Music gay,
Brown-skin steppers
In a cabaret.

White folks, laugh!
White folks, pray!

"Me an' ma baby's
    Got two mo' ways,
Two mo' ways to do de Charleston!"

The Weary Blues

Droning a drowsy syncopated tune,
Rocking back and forth to a mellow croon,
    I heard a Negro play.
Down on Lenox Avenue the other night
By the pale dull pallor of an old gas light
    He did a lazy sway. . . .
    He did a lazy sway. . . .
To the tune o' those Weary Blues.
With his ebony hands on each ivory key
He made that poor piano moan with melody.
    O Blues!
Swaying to and fro on his rickety stool
He played that sad raggy tune like a musical fool.
    Sweet Blues!
Coming from a black man's soul.
    O Blues!
In a deep song voice with a melancholy tone
I heard that Negro sing, that old piano moan—
    "Ain't got nobody in all this world,
    Ain't got nobody but ma self.
    I's gwine to quit ma frownin'
    And put ma troubles on de shelf."
Thump, thump, thump, went his foot on the floor.
He played a few chords then he sang some more—
    "I got de Weary Blues
    And I can't be satisfied.

Got de Weary Blues
And can't be satisfied
I ain't happy no mo'
And I wish that I had died."
And far into the night he crooned that tune.
The stars went out and so did the moon.
The singer stopped playing and went to bed.
While the Weary Blues echoed through his head
He slept like a rock or a man that's dead.

Homesick Blues

De railroad bridge's
A sad song in de air.
De railroad bridge's
A sad song in de air.
Ever time de trains pass
I wants to go somewhere.

I went down to de station.
Ma heart was in ma mouth.
Went down to de station.
Heart was in ma mouth.
Lookin' for a box car
To roll me to de South.

Homesick blues, Lawd,
'S a terrible thing to have.
Homesick blues is
A terrible thing to have.
To keep from cryin'
I opens ma mouth an' laughs.

Wide River

Ma baby lives across de river
An' I ain't got no boat.
She lives across de river.
I ain't got no boat.
I ain't a good swimmer
An' I don't know how to float.

Wide, wide river
'Twixt ma love an' me.
Wide, wide river
'Twixt ma love an' me.
I never knowed how
Wide a river can be.

Got to cross that river
An' git to ma baby somehow.
Cross that river,
Git to ma baby somehow—
Cause if I don't see ma baby
I'll lay down an' die right now.

Minstrel Man

Because my mouth
Is wide with laughter
And my throat
Is deep with song,
You do not think
I suffer after
I have held my pain
So long?

Because my mouth
Is wide with laughter,
You do not hear
My inner cry?
Because my feet
Are gay with dancing,
You do not know
I die?

A Black Pierrot

I am a black Pierrot:
   She did not love me,
   So I crept away into the night
   And the night was black, too.

I am a black Pierrot:
   She did not love me,
   So I wept until the red dawn
   Dripped blood over the eastern hills
   And my heart was bleeding, too.

I am a black Pierrot:
   She did not love me,
   So with my once gay-colored soul
   Shrunken like a balloon without air,
   I went forth in the morning
   To seek a new brown love.

Bound No'th Blues

Goin' down de road, Lawd,
Goin' down de road.
Down de road, Lawd,
Way, way down de road.
Got to find somebody
To help me carry dis load.

Road's in front o' me,
Nothin' to do but walk.
Road's in front o' me,
Walk . . . and walk . . . and walk.
I'd like to meet a good friend
To come along an' talk.

Hates to be lonely,
Lawd, I hates to be sad.
Says I hates to be lonely,
Hates to be lonely an' sad,
But ever friend you finds seems
Like they try to do you bad.

Road, road, road, O!
Road, road . . . road . . . road, road!
Road, road, road, O!
On de No'thern road.
These Mississippi towns ain't
Fit fer a hoppin' toad.

Song

Lovely, dark, and lonely one,
Bare your bosom to the sun.
Do not be afraid of light,
You who are a child of night.

Open wide your arms to life,
Whirl in the wind of pain and strife,
Face the wall with the dark closed gate,
Beat with bare, brown fists—
And wait.

Passing Love

Because you are to me a song
I must not sing you over-long.

Because you are to me a prayer
I cannot say you everywhere.

Because you are to me a rose—
You will not stay when summer goes.

When Sue Wears Red

When Susanna Jones wears red
Her face is like an ancient cameo
Turned brown by the ages.

Come with a blast of trumpets,
    Jesus!

When Susanna Jones wears red
A queen from some time-dead Egyptian night
Walks once again.

Blow trumpets, Jesus!

And the beauty of Susanna Jones in red
Burns in my heart a love-fire sharp like pain.

Sweet silver trumpets,
    Jesus!

43

Po' Boy Blues

When I was home de
Sunshine seemed like gold.
When I was home de
Sunshine seemed like gold.
Since I come up North de
Whole wide world's turned cold.

I was a good boy,
Never done no wrong.
Yes, I was a good boy,
Never done no wrong,
But this world is weary
An' de road is hard an' long.

I fell in love with
A gal I thought was kind.
Fell in love with
A gal I thought was kind.
She made me lose ma money
An' almost lose ma mind.

Weary, weary,
Weary early in de morn.
Weary, weary,
Early, early in de morn.
I's so weary
I wish I'd never been born.

Song for a Banjo Dance

Shake your brown feet, honey,
Shake your brown feet, chile,
Shake your brown feet, honey,
Shake 'em swift and wil'—
    Get way back, honey,
    Do that rockin' step.
    Slide on over, darling,
        Now! Come out
        With your left.
Shake your brown feet, honey,
Shake 'em, honey chile.

Sun's going down this evening—
Might never rise no mo'.
The sun's going down this very night—
Might never rise no mo'—
So dance with swift feet, honey,
    (The banjo's sobbing low)
Dance with swift feet, honey—
    Might never dance no mo'.

Shake your brown feet, Liza,
Shake 'em, Liza, chile,
Shake your brown feet, Liza,
    (The music's soft and wil')
Shake your brown feet, Liza,

(The banjo's sobbing low)
The sun's going down this very night—
Might never rise no mo'.

Night and Morn

Sun's a settin',
This is what I'm gonna sing.
Sun's a settin',
This is what I'm gonna sing:
I feels de blues a comin',
Wonder what de blues'll bring?

Sun's a risin',
This is gonna be ma song.
Sun's a risin',
This is gonna be ma song:
I could be blue but
I been blue all night long.

FEET O' JESUS

Feet o' Jesus

At de feet o' Jesus,
Sorrow like a sea.
Lordy, let yo' mercy
Come driftin' down on me.

At de feet o' Jesus,
At yo' feet I stand.
O, ma precious Jesus,
Please reach out yo' hand.

Sinner

Have mercy, Lord!

Po' an' bowed
An' humble an' lonesome
An' a sinner in yo' sight.

Have mercy, Lord!

Prayer

I ask you this:
Which way to go?
I ask you this:
Which sin to bear?
Which crown to put
Upon my hair?
I do not know,
Lord God,
I do not know.

Judgment Day

They put ma body in de ground,
My soul went flyin' o' de town.

Lord Jesus!

Went flyin' to de stars an' moon
A shoutin' God, I's comin' soon.

O Jesus!

Lord in heaben,
Crown on His head,
Says don't be 'fraid
Cause you ain't dead.

Kind Jesus!

An' now I'm settin' clean an' bright
In de sweet o' ma Lord's sight,—
  Clean an' bright,
    Clean an' bright.

Ma Lord

Ma Lord ain't no stuck-up man.
Ma Lord, he ain't proud.
When he goes a-walkin'
He gives me his hand.
"You ma friend," he 'lowed.

Ma Lord knowed what it was to work.
He knowed how to pray.
Ma Lord's life was trouble, too,
Trouble ever day.

Ma Lord ain't no stuck-up man.
He's a friend o' mine.
When He went to heaben,
His soul on fire,
He tole me I was gwine.
He said, "Sho you'll come wid Me
An' be ma friend through eternity."

Baby

Albert!
Hey, Albert!
Don't you play in dat road.
  You see dem trucks
  A goin' by.
  One run ovah you
  An' you die.
Albert, don't you play in dat road.

Lullaby

(For a Black Mother)

My little dark baby,
My little earth-thing,
My little love-one,
What shall I sing
For your lullaby?

Stars,
Stars,
A necklace of stars
Winding the night.

My little black baby,
My dark body's baby,
What shall I sing
For your lullaby?

Moon,
Moon,
Great diamond moon,
Kissing the night.

Oh, little dark baby,
Night black baby,

Stars, stars,
Moon,
Night stars,
Moon,

For your sleep-song lullaby!

Prayer Meeting

Glory! Halleluiah!
De dawn's a-comin'!
Glory! Halleluiah!
De dawn's a-comin'!
A black old woman croons
In the amen-corner of the
Ebecanezer Baptist Church.
A black old woman croons—
De dawn's a-comin'!

WALKERS WITH THE DAWN

Walkers with the Dawn

Being walkers with the dawn and morning,
Walkers with the sun and morning,
We are not afraid of night,
Nor days of gloom,
Nor darkness—
Being walkers with the sun and morning.

63

African Dance

The low beating of the tom-toms,
The slow beating of the tom-toms,
  Low . . . slow
  Slow . . . low—
Stirs your blood.

  Dance!
A night-veiled girl
  Whirls softly into a
  Circle of light.
  Whirls softly . . . slowly,
Like a wisp of smoke around the fire—
  And the tom-toms beat,
  And the tom-toms beat,
And the low beating of the tom-toms
  Stirs your blood.

Aunt Sue's Stories

Aunt Sue has a head full of stories.
Aunt Sue has a whole heart full of stories.
Summer nights on the front porch
Aunt Sue cuddles a brown-faced child to her bosom
And tells him stories.

Black slaves
Working in the hot sun,
And black slaves
Walking in the dewy night,
And black slaves
Singing sorrow songs on the banks of a mighty river
Mingle themselves softly
In the flow of old Aunt Sue's voice,
Mingle themselves softly
In the dark shadows that cross and recross
Aunt Sue's stories.

And the dark-faced child, listening,
Knows that Aunt Sue's stories are real stories.
He knows that Aunt Sue
Never got her stories out of any book at all,
But that they came
Right out of her own life.

And the dark-faced child is quiet
Of a summer night
Listening to Aunt Sue's stories.

Alabama Earth

(At Booker Washington's grave)

Deep in Alabama earth
His buried body lies—
But higher than the singing pines
And taller than the skies
And out of Alabama earth
To all the world there goes
The truth a simple heart has held
And the strength a strong hand knows,
While over Alabama earth
These words are gently spoken:
Serve—and hate will die unborn.
Love—and chains are broken.

My People

The night is beautiful,
So the faces of my people.

The stars are beautiful,
So the eyes of my people.

Beautiful, also, is the sun.
Beautiful, also, are the souls of my people.

67

Lincoln Monument: Washington

Let's go see old Abe
Sitting in the marble and the moonlight,
Sitting lonely in the marble and the moonlight,
Quiet for ten thousand centuries, old Abe.
Quiet for a million, million years.

Quiet—

And yet a voice forever
Against the
Timeless walls
Of time—
Old Abe.

Dream Variation

To fling my arms wide
In some place of the sun,
To whirl and to dance
Till the white day is done.
Then rest at cool evening
Beneath a tall tree
While night comes on gently,
  Dark like me—
That is my dream!

To fling my arms wide
In the face of the sun,
Dance! Whirl! Whirl!
Till the quick day is done.
Rest at pale evening. . . .
A tall, slim tree. . . .
Night coming tenderly
  Black like me.

Sun Song

Sun and softness,
Sun and the beaten hardness of the earth,
Sun and the song of all the sun-stars
Gathered together—
Dark ones of Africa,
I bring you my songs
To sing on the Georgia roads.

The Negro Speaks of Rivers

I've known rivers:
I've known rivers ancient as the world and older than the
      flow of human blood in human veins.

My soul has grown deep like the rivers.

I bathed in the Euphrates when dawns were young.
I built my hut near the Congo and it lulled me to sleep.
I looked upon the Nile and raised the pyramids above it.
I heard the singing of the Mississippi when Abe Lincoln
      went down to New Orleans, and I've seen its
      muddy bosom turn all golden in the sunset.

I've known rivers:
Ancient, dusky rivers.

My soul has grown deep like the rivers.

The Negro

I am a Negro:
  Black as the night is black,
  Black like the depths of my Africa.

I've been a slave:
  Caesar told me to keep his door-steps clean.
  I brushed the boots of Washington.

I've been a worker:
  Under my hand the pyramids arose.
  I made mortar for the Woolworth Building.

I've been a singer:
  All the way from Africa to Georgia
  I carried my sorrow songs.
  I made ragtime.

I've been a victim:
  The Belgians cut off my hands in the Congo.
  They lynch me now in Texas.

I am a Negro:
  Black as the night is black.
  Black like the depths of my Africa.

Mother to Son

Well, son, I'll tell you:
Life for me ain't been no crystal stair.
It's had tacks in it,
And splinters,
And boards torn up,
And places with no carpet on the floor—
Bare.
But all the time
I'se been a-climbin' on,
And reachin' landin's,
And turnin' corners,
And sometimes goin' in the dark
Where there ain't been no light.
So, boy, don't you turn back.
Don't you set down on the steps
'Cause you finds it kinder hard.
Don't you fall now—
For I'se still goin', honey,
I'se still climbin',
And life for me ain't been no crystal stair.

As I Grew Older

It was a long time ago.
I have almost forgotten my dream.
But it was there then,
In front of me,
Bright like a sun—
My dream.

And then the wall rose,
Rose slowly,
Slowly,
Between me and my dream.
Rose slowly, slowly,
Dimming,
Hiding,
The light of my dream.
Rose until it touched the sky—
The wall.

Shadow.
I am black.

I lie down in the shadow.
No longer the light of my dream before me,
Above me.
Only the thick wall.
Only the shadow.

My hands!
My dark hands!
Break through the wall!
Find my dream!
Help me to shatter this darkness,
To smash this night,
To break this shadow
Into a thousand lights of sun,
Into a thousand whirling dreams
Of sun!

I, Too

I, too, sing America.

I am the darker brother.
They send me to eat in the kitchen
When company comes,
But I laugh,
And eat well,
And grow strong.

Tomorrow,
I'll sit at the table
When company comes.
Nobody'll dare
Say to me,
"Eat in the kitchen,"
Then.

Besides,
They'll see how beautiful I am
And be ashamed—

I, too, am America.

Youth

We have tomorrow
Bright before us
Like a flame.

Yesterday
A night-gone thing,
A sun-down name.

And dawn-today
Broad arch above the road we came.

We march!

I was born
He, my brother was born